A Note t

DK READERS is a compelling program for beginning readers, designed in conjunction with leading literacy experts, including Dr. Linda Gambrell, Professor of Education at Clemson University. Dr. Gambrell has served as President of the National Reading Conference and the College Reading Association, and has recently been elected to serve as President of the International Reading Association.

Beautiful illustrations and superb full-color photographs combine with engaging, easy-to-read stories to offer a fresh approach to each subject in the series. Each DK READER is guaranteed to capture a child's interest while developing his or her reading skills, general knowledge, and love of reading.

The five levels of DK READERS are aimed at different reading abilities, enabling you to choose the books that are exactly right for your child:

Pre-level 1: Learning to read
Level 1: Beginning to read
Level 2: Beginning to read alone
Level 3: Reading alone
Level 4: Proficient readers

The "normal" age at which a child begins to read can be anywhere from three to eight years old. Adult participation through the lower levels is very helpful for providing encouragement, discussing storylines, and sounding out unfamiliar words.

No matter which level you select, you can be sure that you are helping your child learn to read, then read to learn!

LONDON, NEW YORK, MUNICH,
MELBOURNE, AND DELHI

Editorial Lead Heather Jones
Special Sales Manager Silvia La Greca
Associate Publisher Nigel Duffield

Reading Consultant
Linda Gambrell, Ph.D.

Produced by
Shoreline Publishing Group LLC
President James Buckley, Jr.
Designer Tom Carling, carlingdesign.com

The Boy Scouts of America®, Cub Scouts®,
Boys' Life®, and rank insignia are registered
trademarks of the Boy Scouts of America.
Printed under license from the
Boy Scouts of America.

First American Edition, 2008
08 09 10 11 10 9 8 7 6 5 4 3 2 1
Published in the United States by DK Publishing
375 Hudson Street, New York, New York 10014

Published in Great Britain by Dorling Kindersley Limited

DK books are available at special discounts when purchased in bulk
for sales promotions, premiums, fund-raising, or educational use.
For details, contact:
DK Publishing Special Markets, 375 Hudson St., New York, NY 10014
SpecialSales@dk.com

A catalog record for this book is available
from the Library of Congress.
ISBN: 978-07566-44192 (Paperback)

Printed and bound in China by L. Rex Printing Co. LTD.

The publisher would like to thank the following for their kind
permission to reproduce their photographs:
(Key: a=above; b=below/bottom; c=center; l=left; r=right; t=top)
AP/Wide World: 31; Corbis: 29t, 30tl; Dreamstime.com: 14b, 15t, 16b, 18b, 19b,
20tl, 23br, 41br, 42bl; iStock: 4tl, 7t, 7b, 10bl, 18tl, 29br, 30b, 34b, 41, 44tr, 45tr;
Photos.com: 13t, 25br, 27tr, 35t, 36tl

All other images © Dorling Kindersley Limited.
For more information see: www.dkimages.com

Discover more at
www.dk.com

Contents

 **READERS**

Boys' Life SERIES
Secrets of
Snakes

Written by Kathryn Stevens

DK Publishing

Creatures of legend

Slithering, scaly snakes are many people's worst nightmare. TV shows and movies often show snakes as deadly, sinister creatures. When moviemakers want to create a sense of danger, snakes are a perfect choice! What could be scarier than falling into a pit of wriggling vipers, wrestling a giant anaconda, or staring into the eyes of a coiled cobra just as it's ready to strike? It's no wonder snakes have such a bad reputation!

All over the world, and all through history, snakes or serpents have been part of people's religions, beliefs, and

Eden snake
In the Bible's story of Adam and Eve in the Garden of Eden, a snake brings evil into the world.

Snake story
According to Irish legend, St. Patrick chased the snakes out of Ireland. Actually, there weren't any snakes living in Ireland.

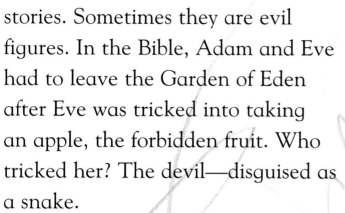

stories. Sometimes they are evil figures. In the Bible, Adam and Eve had to leave the Garden of Eden after Eve was tricked into taking an apple, the forbidden fruit. Who tricked her? The devil—disguised as a snake.

In Greek mythology, Medusa was a woman with squirming snakes on her head instead of hair. One look at her could turn a person to stone. A hero named Perseus killed her by using his shield as a mirror. The mirror kept him from looking directly at Medusa as he chopped off her head.

Snakes everywhere
There are at least 2,700 different kinds, or species, of snakes. Snakes live in every part of the world except places that are very cold.

Krishna
In Hindu stories, the god Krishna (right) defeated the evil snake Kaliya in a battle by a river.

Snake story
Milk snakes got their name because people thought they snuck into sheds and barns to steal milk from cows. Actually, the snakes were hunting mice.

In ancient Egypt, people believed that a gigantic, evil snake named Apep ruled the darkness and was the enemy of the sun. In India, people believed that a snake called Rahu swallowed the sun and moon.

But other beliefs and stories about snakes take a more positive view. Snakes appear in many stories of how the world was created. They appear as guardians of the underworld. In some places they are viewed as lucky, or associated with healing. Sometimes they are associated with rainfall or good harvests. In fact, in some regions, people dedicate shrines or temples to snakes.

Despite their sometimes fearsome reputation, snakes are an important part of the natural world. They eat huge numbers of insects and animal pests, including mice and rats. And most of them pose no danger at all to humans.

Death by snake Ancient accounts say that Cleopatra, the Egyptian queen, killed herself with the bite of an asp.

Charming Snake charmers play music while their snakes seem to dance along. But the snakes can't even hear music. They're just following the movements of the snake charmer's body and flute.

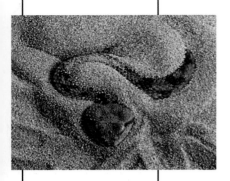

A kind of reptile

Snakes belong to the animal group called reptiles. Turtles, tortoises, lizards, alligators, and crocodiles are reptiles, too. Reptiles are air-breathing animals with backbones and bony skeletons. Their bodies are usually covered with hard scales or plates. On snakes, the scales overlap. Stretchy skin between the scales lets a snake bend and flex its body freely. The scales hold moisture in the animal's body.

Hiding out
Sand vipers wriggle down into the desert sand until only their heads show. That keeps them cool and helps them ambush their prey.

Lots of neighbors
In the Narcisse Wildlife Management Area in Manitoba, Canada, thousands of red-sided garter snakes hibernate together through the cold winter.

Basking in the sun for warmth

That's especially important for snakes that live in hot, dry regions. The tough scales also protect the snake from injuries.

Reptiles are known as "cold-blooded" animals. That means that they don't warm their bodies with energy from the food they eat. Instead, they rely on outside heat. If they get too cold, their bodies slow down, and their digestive systems can't break down food. To warm up, snakes in many regions bask in the sun or flatten their bodies against a warm surface. In places with cold winters, they might hibernate for several months. Sometimes hundreds—or even thousands—of snakes hibernate together! But snakes can get too hot, too. Desert snakes usually hide from the heat of the day.

Scaly stuff
Snakes' scales are made mostly of keratin, the same substance that makes up cow's horns and your hair and fingernails.

Firmly attached
Fish scales come off without damaging the skin, but a snake's scales are actually part of its skin.

Amazing bodies

What makes snakes different from other reptiles? Their long, tubelike body shape and lack of legs. To match their body shape, snakes have some long, slender organs on the inside. A snake's throat, or gullet, can be about one-third of its body length. Beyond that is a long, thin stomach. Both the gullet and the stomach can stretch wide to take in a big meal.

Despite their slim bodies and small heads, snakes have an amazing ability to swallow their prey whole. Their mouths can stretch wide. Backward-pointing teeth keep prey from slipping out. The snake moves the bones of its jaws a little at a time, slowly "walking" them along the body of its prey.

Some types of snakes have thinner bodies than others. Snakes

Keep breathing
It's hard to breathe when your mouth is wrapped around a huge egg or a whole gazelle! A snake can push its windpipe forward, so it stays open despite a big mouthful of food.

Big mouth
Snakes like this green tree snake can open their jaws many times wider than their body to grab prey.

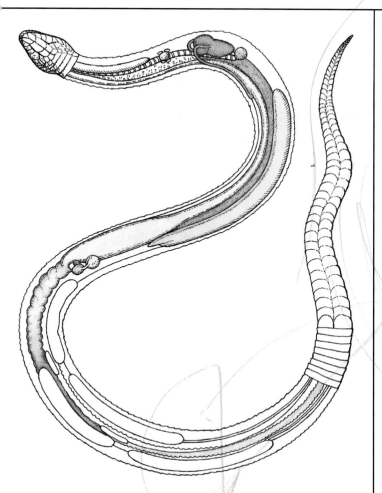

This cutaway drawing shows how many snakes' internal organs are arranged. They are long and thin, like the snake. The top yellow part is the liver, and the red part the heart. The blue shows the stomach and intestines.

that live in trees tend to have thin, light bodies to move through trees easily, with long tails for hanging onto branches. Snakes that chase their prey in open country tend to be long and thin, too. Heavier, thicker snakes hunt by lying in wait.

Lookalikes
Some burrowing lizards are legless and look very much like snakes.

11

Open wide!
A snake's jaw can unhinge and open very, very wide. This lets the snake swallow prey that is actually larger than its own body!

Bony
Snake skeletons include the skull at the top, the backbone or spine along the whole length . . . and dozens and dozens of ribs!

Moving without legs

A snake's long body has lots of backbones, or vertebrae, with ribs attached to them. Muscles fastened to the ribs can bend and twist the snake's body in any direction.

Snakes move by anchoring some points on their bodies and moving the rest. They move in different ways. Some snakes use "serpentine" motion, bending in a gentle **S** shape. The sides of their bodies push against bumps on the ground to move them along. In burrows or other narrow spaces, snakes often

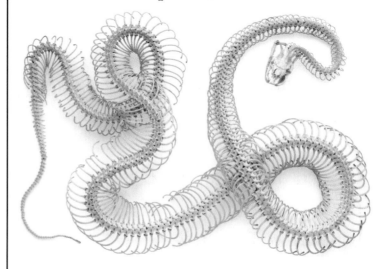

move by "concertina" motion. The snake bunches up the back of its body and braces it against the walls of the burrow. Then it pushes the front end forward. Next it bunches up the front end and pulls its tail forward toward its front end.

Some snakes, especially bigger, heavier ones, creep along in a straight line, moving sort of like caterpillars. They use their belly scales to grab the ground. They move forward by tightening and relaxing their muscles in waves.

Bendable bodies
Depending on their species and size, snakes can have 180 to over 400 vertebrae like these. People have only 32.

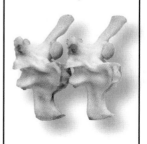

13

Desert snake
Sidewinders like these are found in the hot, dry desert areas of the American Southwest.

Not so fast
Green mambas have been measured moving 7 miles (11 km) per hour. Somewhat faster speeds have been reported for snakes but are hard to measure.

In soft sand, some snakes move by "sidewinding." They throw their bodies sideways in a spiral, with only a few body parts on the ground. That helps the snakes move. It also keeps them off the hot sand. Some snakes swim very well, even without fins or legs to push them through the water. They use serpentine movement to swim, curving their bodies into an S shape, back and forth in the water. Garter snakes are good swimmers. Sometimes they even catch and eat fish. Sea snakes have flattened tails that help them swim.

Many snakes climb very well. Tree snakes hold on to branches with their tails while they pull their bodies higher.

Flying snakes are tree-climbers that don't really fly, but they glide very well. These hunters climb through trees in southern Asia, jumping from branch to branch as they search for lizards and frogs. They can glide from higher branches to lower ones, flattening their stomachs to trap air and slow their fall. As they glide, they turn and twist their bodies to steer.

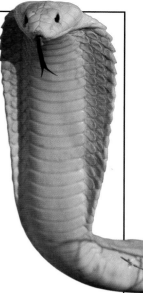

On the attack
A cobra can move forward even with the front of its body raised off the ground, ready to strike.

Nerve center
This cutaway drawing shows the parts of the snake's brain, including the sense organs and inner ears.

A fixed stare
Snakes always seem to be staring. That's because they don't have movable eyelids. Instead, their eyes are protected by a clear scale called a spectacle.

Snake senses

Snakes have very good senses to help them find their way around, stay safe, and hunt their prey. Their senses are different from ours, though. They don't have ears or earholes on the outsides of their bodies. Instead, when their heads are on the ground, they "hear" as vibrations move through their jawbones and skulls to their inner ears.

How good is their eyesight? That depends on the snake's way of life and where it lives. Snakes that burrow underground usually have poor eyesight. Many snakes that hunt in the daytime have good vision, especially for things that move. Some snakes even have binocular vision, with both eyes pointing forward, like those on people. Binocular vision helps animals judge distances accurately.

That's especially helpful for snakes that move from branch to branch and catch their prey in trees.

Snakes "taste" their environment as well as smell it. When snakes flick their tongues, the tongues pick up tiny particles from their surroundings, including the air. Inside the snakes' mouths, special "Jacobson's organs" help the snakes smell and taste these particles to learn what is around them. Snakes use this ability to find and taste foods, find mates, and avoid enemies.

Heat detectors
Pit vipers (including rattlesnakes) and some boas and pythons have "heat pits" that sense heat from other animals. These snakes can find and strike warm-blooded prey even in the dark.

Snake science
Ludwig Levin Jacobson was a Danish scientist in the early 1800s. He published a paper in 1811 that first identified the part of a snake that helps it "taste" its environment.

Silent killers

Snakes are predators that hunt and kill other animals for food. Different types of snakes eat prey ranging from ants and termites to large animals such as gazelles.

Different snakes have different ways of hunting, too. Many hunt

Follow me
Slug- and snail-eating snakes hunt down their victims by tracking their trails of slime.

Spot the snake!
Can you see the Gaboon viper hiding in this pile of leaves? Here's a hint: Look for a dark stripe on a gray background. Got it? Now back up slowly!

by ambush—hiding and waiting for their prey to come to them. Vipers, pythons, and some types of boas are ambush hunters. Camouflage helps them hide until prey wanders near. For example, vine snakes in Southeast Asia look like thin green vines hanging from branches. They stay still and hidden, waiting for lizards to wander close.

Other snakes are more active hunters, seeking out and catching their prey. Whipsnakes and racers can move fast to chase their prey along the ground. Green tree snakes chase their prey in the trees. They climb very well, and their thin, green bodies blend in with leaves, branches, and vines. They slither through the trees looking for birds, frogs, or lizards.

Snake or tree?
Green tree snakes blend into the branches of a tree, waiting for prey to come near.

Going fishing?
Some snakes have specially colored tails that they use as lures. They wiggle their tails and when a fish comes to look, the snake grabs it.

Snakes also have different ways of killing their prey. Some just catch their prey and swallow it—still alive! That works best if the animal is small and harmless, like a frog.

Constrictors kill their prey before eating it. They grab the animal, hold it with their sharp teeth, wrap themselves around its body, and squeeze. But constrictors don't crush their victims—they suffocate them. Every time the animal breathes out, the snake tightens its hold a little. The animal finds it harder and harder to breathe—and soon it can't breathe at all. When the snake feels the animal's heart stop beating, it relaxes its grip. Then the snake opens its

Tight spaces
Australia's woma pythons hunt their prey in underground burrows where there isn't room to coil around them. Instead, they "constrict" prey by pressing the animals against burrow walls.

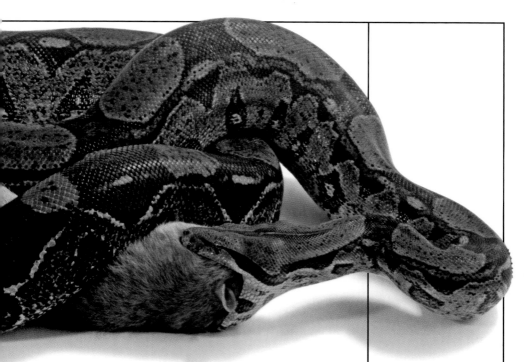

jaws wide and pulls the animal in, usually starting with the head.

Digesting a big meal can take days or even longer. Afterward, the snake doesn't need to eat again for a while. Because snakes don't need food energy to warm their bodies, they don't need as much food as mammals and other warm-blooded animals. Some constrictors go for weeks between meals. After a really huge meal, some snakes go for a year without eating!

The big squeeze
Boas and pythons are all constrictors. Anacondas are boas that live in rivers in South America.

Big meal
A year without eating? Well, if a snake has managed to swallow a gazelle or small deer, that would let them last that long.

This rattler is
ready to strike.
You can see
drops of venom
hanging from
its fangs.

Big and deadly
King cobras
are the longest
venomous
snakes. Some
are more than
16 feet (5 m)
long! The
venom from
one bite can kill
an elephant—
or 20 people.

Deadly poisons

Some snakes use poisonous
venom to kill their prey—and to
defend themselves. They have sacs
of venom near two sharp, hollow
fangs. When they bite, they inject
venom into their victims through
the fangs. Venom is a poisonous
kind of saliva (the moisture in an
animal's—or person's—mouth).
Venoms of different snakes have
different ingredients. Some attack
the victim's nerves so the animal

can't move—or breathe. Some work on the blood, causing bleeding. Some break down the victim's flesh. Sea snakes produce venom that attacks the muscles.

Most poisonous snakes, such as cobras, have fangs in the fronts of their mouths. They strike their prey quickly and then often let go, to avoid getting hurt as the victim struggles. Even if the victim moves away, the snake can track it down. Vipers' front fangs are extra long and fold up out of the way when they're not being used. Rattlesnakes are vipers with folding front fangs. Some other venomous snakes, such as mangrove snakes, have their fangs at the backs of their jaws instead of the front. They hold onto their prey and chew on it to inject their venom.

Venom vein
A snake's fangs are hollow. The venom flows from a gland in their head out from the pointed end of a fang.

Sea death
Sea snakes have very strong venom. It acts quickly, to kill fish before they can swim away.

Small but deadly
Baby snakes are just as venomous as adults—and often more aggressive. A cobra can kill from the moment it hatches.

Milking snakes
Scientists working to make medicine to help snake-bite victims need snake venom. To get it, they (carefully!) make a snake put out venom in a process called "milking."

Of the more than 800 kinds of poisonous snakes, only 250 or so are dangerous to humans. Venomous snakes live in many parts of the world, but deadlier ones tend to live in tropical regions. When venomous snakes defend themselves, they don't want to waste their venom, so they usually don't use it unless they really need to.

How do you treat a snakebite? Oddly enough, the best treatment is medicine made from snake venom! Venom "milked" from poisonous snakes is used to make an "antivenom" that helps counteract the venom's effects.

In North America, only a few people a year die from snakebites. That's because poisonous snakes aren't common, people usually wear shoes, and medical treatment is nearby. But in some places where snakes are plentiful, many people go barefoot and medical treatment isn't close. There, snakebite deaths are more common. How many people die from snakebite? Some people estimate 25,000 deaths per year, many of them in India and Burma. Other people think the number is higher.

Down under
Most of Australia's snakes are venomous. One bite from an Australian taipan has enough venom to kill almost a quarter of a million mice.

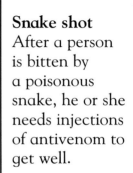

Snake shot
After a person is bitten by a poisonous snake, he or she needs injections of antivenom to get well.

Venom for dinner
Do snakes eat other snakes? And won't they be poisoned if they do? Yes, some snakes do eat other snakes. Some kingsnakes eat rattlesnakes. However, they are not bothered by the rattlers' venom.

Hero
In Rudyard Kipling's *A Jungle Book*, a mongoose named Rikki-Tikki-Tavi saves his human family from deadly cobras.

Snake survival

Snakes might be killers, but plenty of animals kill snakes, too! Even deadly venom isn't always enough to protect snakes from danger. Many birds of prey such as hawks, eagles, and storks eat snakes. So do mammals such as raccoons, skunks, and foxes. Some frogs, lizards, spiders, and insects—and other snakes—eat snakes!

Mongooses are sharp-toothed mammals skilled at killing snakes, even king cobras. With lightning-fast movements, a mongoose avoids the

This series of drawings shows how a lightning-quick mongoose battles a cobra.

snake's strikes and grabs it by the head or the back of the neck. The mongoose's thick fur helps protect it. People brought mongooses to the West Indies to kill rats and snakes. Unfortunately, the mongooses did too well there, turning into pests themselves.

Africa's secretary birds have the longest legs of any bird of prey, and they use them to kill snakes—including cobras. They kick the snake just behind the head or stomp on it, using their wings to keep the snake from being able to strike. People have reported seeing these birds drop or throw snakes to the ground to kill them.

Snake bird
The wide-winged secretary bird shows off its long legs. It gets its name from the pointy feathers on its head, which looked like quill pens used by office workers in the 1800s.

Bad and good
"Red next to yellow, kill a fellow. Red next to black, okay for Jack." Now, look at these pictures and see which is the deadly coral snake and which is a harmless milk snake.

Is it dead? No!
European grass snakes roll over and wriggle to look as if they are dying. Then they play dead, with their mouths open and their tongues hanging out.

Snakes have lots of ways of trying to stay safe. The easiest way is simply to hide. Camouflage protects many snakes by breaking up the outlines of their bodies and hiding them against their surroundings. Snakes' flexible bodies can also squeeze into hiding spots or hide by looking like hanging vines.

Other snakes have very different protective coloring. Some snakes, such as venomous coral snakes and harmless milk snakes, have brightly colored bands that seem to discourage enemies. Some

A good disguise
Some snakes have tails that look a lot like heads. When in danger, these snakes move their tails as if they were heads—even pretending to strike.

scientists think the harmless snakes are imitating the coloring of the poisonous snakes. Others think both types are taking advantage of a tendency for predators to avoid brightly colored prey.

If hiding doesn't work, many snakes try to escape. If they are cornered, they often curl themselves into a tight ball, with their head at the center. Some do aggressive displays to scare their enemies. They might puff up their bodies, hiss, open their mouths wide, or look as if they are about to strike.

Keep away!
Rattlesnakes warn enemies by shaking the rattles on their tails. The rattles are made of hollow sections of keratin that click together.

Spitting cobras
When spitting cobras hunt, they inject venom with a bite. But to defend themselves, some can spray venom almost 10 feet (3 m)! The spray causes pain and even blindness.

A big show
Cobras spread their necks to look bigger and more frightening. "Eye" markings on the back help scare enemies, too.

Even deadly venom and clever camouflage can't protect snakes from their most dangerous enemies—humans. People sometimes kill snakes because they fear them or view them as pests. Sometimes they kill them for sport. Some snakes are hunted so their skins can be made into boots, purses, or wallets. Wild snakes are captured and transported illegally to sell as pets. Often they die from poor care or improper handling.

Many snakes are run over by cars as they cross roads or bask on the warm surface of the roadway. Others are killed by animals such as cats, dogs, rats, and mongooses that people have released where those animals don't belong.

But the biggest threat to most snakes is loss of their habitat, or the places where they live. Logging, farming, and building are destroying many wilderness areas where snakes live. Unlike birds or many mammals, snakes have an especially hard time escaping from such challenges. Habitat changes tied to global warming are a big concern, too.

Snake cowboy
At rattlesnake roundups like this one in Georgia, experts trap snakes that they find near homes and towns. The snakes are then released into the wild.

How many?
The number of eggs in a nestful, or clutch, varies. Some snakes only lay a few eggs. Some kinds can lay a hundred or more.

Nesting spot
Compost is rotting plant matter. Many people have compost piles to make new soil. Snakes sometimes make their nests in these compost piles.

Starting out small

Most snakes lay eggs. The shells of snakes' eggs aren't hard like those of birds' eggs. Instead, they're mostly soft and leathery. Usually female snakes hide and protect their eggs by burying them in soft sand or under a little soil. Rotting plant matter produces heat, so snakes sometimes lay their eggs in dead plant matter to keep them warm.

After laying their eggs, most snakes leave them alone. Pythons and a few other snakes curl themselves around their eggs to protect them. Some pythons even shiver to keep the eggs a little warmer.

A snake egg gets larger as its absorbs moisture from its surroundings. Inside the egg, the young snake keeps developing— and getting bigger. The snake ends up tightly curled inside the egg. Sometimes it is hard to believe that such a long snake could fit inside such a small egg!

Snake-shaped
Ground pythons and African grand snakes lay eggs that look like long tubes, instead of the rounder eggs of most snakes.

Is it done yet?
How long does it take for snakes' eggs to hatch? That depends on the species— and also on the egg's temperature. Some eggs take up to three months.

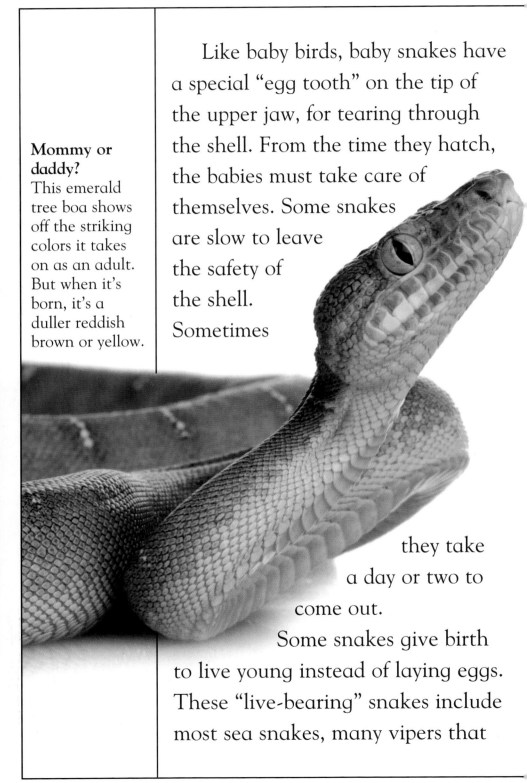

Mommy or daddy?
This emerald tree boa shows off the striking colors it takes on as an adult. But when it's born, it's a duller reddish brown or yellow.

Like baby birds, baby snakes have a special "egg tooth" on the tip of the upper jaw, for tearing through the shell. From the time they hatch, the babies must take care of themselves. Some snakes are slow to leave the safety of the shell. Sometimes they take a day or two to come out.

Some snakes give birth to live young instead of laying eggs. These "live-bearing" snakes include most sea snakes, many vipers that live in cold regions, and many tree-dwelling snakes. Snakes such as these live in places where it would be hard to keep eggs warm and safe.

Instead of developing within eggs, these babies develop inside thin coverings, or membranes, within the mother's body. They break through the membranes when they are born.

Baby snakes look very much like their parents, but much smaller. Sometimes they're a different color, though. Emerald tree boas are yellow or reddish brown when they're born. The change color as they grow, becoming green by the time they're a year old. Other snakes keep the same look and color, but grow longer and larger.

Wet snake
Sea snakes, which live underwater and do not lay eggs, are among the world's deadliest snakes.

Baby rattlers
Rattlesnakes are live-bearers. As soon as the babies are born, they're on their own.

Are you blue?
This Wagler's viper, or temple viper, is one of the most unusually colored snakes, with a strong blue tint.

Slippery
When snakes shed, an oily substance between their old skin and their new skin helps the old skin slide off. Hikers can find snake skins in the wild.

Growing long

Many kinds of animals stop growing when they reach their adult size, but snakes keep growing. Some grow very slowly as they get older and bigger. But others, like pythons, keep growing larger until the day they die.

As snakes get bigger, they outgrow their skin, so they simply shed the old, worn-out one and uncover a new, larger one! Baby snakes grow quickly. They might shed their skin shortly after they hatch from their eggs, and seven times or so in their first year.

Snakes shed their skin all at once, usually in one piece. The shedding starts at the head. The scales over the snake's eyes look milky a few days beforehand. Then the skin loosens up around the

Ornery
Snakes can be aggressive when they're getting ready to shed.

Rattling on
Every time a rattlesnake sheds its skin, it adds a new section to its rattle. The bigger the rattle, the older the snake is.

mouth, and the snake rubs its head on the ground to peel it back. As its head breaks free, the snake starts to slide out of the skin, turning the whole skin inside out. In perhaps half an hour, the old skin is gone, and the snake is colorful in its shiny new scales. The shed skin might be one-fifth longer than the snake was!

Big snake, big prey
Anacondas like this one hunt and eat large animals such as deer, pigs, and caiman, a relative of the alligator.

How long?
It's hard to measure a snake's length accurately! Live ones wriggle, and dead ones stretch.

Most snakes are under 3 feet (less than 1 m) long. About 300 species are really small—only a foot (30 cm) or less. Snakes of the blind snake family are tiny—only 4 inches (10 cm) long! Snakes that live in cooler areas tend to be smaller. Their bodies warm more quickly than those of larger snakes, and they require less food. Very small snakes eat things like ants and termites.

The biggest snakes are in the boa and python families. Indian pythons can grow to around 20 feet (6 m). Reticulated pythons and green anacondas have been reported to reach nearly 33 feet (10 m). The anacondas have heavier bodies, though, making them the biggest snakes overall—up to 550 pounds (250 kg)! Anacondas live in rivers, where the water helps support their weight. Big anacondas have difficulty moving on land.

Really big snakes need a long time to warm themselves up. That's why they're found only in warmer regions. With their huge, heavy bodies, they can hunt only by ambushing their prey.

Boa facts
All types of boa snakes live in Central and South America. The most well-known is the boa constrictor, which can be up to 15 feet (5 m). However, not all boas are big! Rubber boas grow to only 2.5 feet (75 cm).

Big and blind
Not all blind snakes are small. This giant blind snake lives in southern Africa.

Egg lunch
This picture
shows how an
egg-eater snake
expands its
mouth to eat
its prey.

Scary . . . not!
North
America's
hognose snakes
are completely
harmless—but
you'd never
know that
from the way
they flatten
their necks,
hiss, and strike
when they're
threatened.

Cool snakes

All snakes are interesting, and the closer you study them, the more interesting they are! Here are some kinds that are extra cool.

The common egg-eater of southern Africa eats nothing but birds' eggs. This nearly toothless snake stretches its mouth around the eggs and swallows them whole. Special spines on the snake's backbones break the hard shell. Later, the snake spits out the broken, folded-up shell. Since most birds lay their eggs in the spring, that's when egg-eaters lay their own eggs and find food. For the rest of the year, they don't eat at all.

Sea snakes live in the water, but they need to come to the surface to breathe. They can stay underwater for a couple of hours, though. Sea snakes' bodies end up with too much salt from eating fish. The snakes get rid of the extra salt through a special body part in their mouths.

Sunbeam snakes of China and Southeast Asia spend most of their time underground. There they eat rodents, snakes, and other ground-dwelling animals. In the light, sunbeam snakes have shiny scales that look like oil on water.

The boa constrictor, is one of the best-known snakes of Central and South America. These snakes often grow to a length of 10 feet (3 m). The longest was more than 13 feet (4 m) long!

Bumpy noses
Rhinoceros vipers from Africa get their name from hornlike bumps on their snouts.

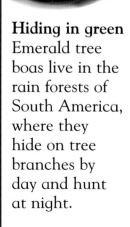

Hiding in green
Emerald tree boas live in the rain forests of South America, where they hide on tree branches by day and hunt at night.

Snakes as pets

Types of pet snakes
- Ball pythons
- Milk snakes
- Rat snakes
- Gopher snakes
- Garter snakes

Glass home
Pet stores sell special snake cages, often made of glass like fish aquariums.

Snakes can make fascinating pets, but they're not for everyone! Snakes need special care and are a big responsibility. Before they decide to get a pet snake, people need to learn a lot about the animals to be able take good care of them. Books and Web sites offer lots of good information on different types of snakes and the care they need. Talking to snake experts can help, too.

What do pet snakes need? They need a safe cage to live in, with fresh air but no escape holes. The cage should be warmer at one end and cooler at the other, so the snake can find just a temperature in which it is comfortable.

Also, snakes like to have a hiding spot where they can curl up

out of sight. They need a shallow water dish and a rock for scraping off their skin when they shed. They also need the right food. Depending on the species, that can mean anything from insects or worms to frozen (or live!) mice.

Snakes should be checked and have their cages cleaned daily, to make sure they're healthy and content. If a snake seems ill, it should go to a veterinarian who works with snakes.

Not too corny
Corn snakes get their name because their color patterning looks like an ear of corn. These harmless snakes come from the eastern United States and grow to 6 feet (less than 2 m) long. They're easy to handle, making them popular as pets.

Snake scientists
People who study snakes and other reptiles and amphibians are called herpetologists.

Keeping in touch
Radio transmitters can send information on a snake's body temperature and location. That helps scientists learn more about how the snake lives.

Helping snakes

People don't usually think of snakes as needing help! But with all the dangers snakes face worldwide, they could use more people working on their behalf. They could use more friends who appreciate what fascinating creatures they are.

There's still a lot we don't know about snakes, and there's a real need for people who want to study them. Education is needed, too, so people understand more about snakes and how they fit into the food chain and the natural world. When people know more about snakes, they become more interested in saving wild populations and the places where they live.

Some progress is being made. Governments and organizations are setting aside land for nature preserves. These protected areas provide homes for the plants and animals—including snakes.

Many zoos are working on programs to help rebuild wild populations of some snakes. New Laws help stop the international trade in wild snakes. But there is still a lot to do! Snakes are certainly worth saving!

Friend or foe? People sometimes think leopard snakes are vipers and kill them. But these snakes are not only harmless, they're helpful. They often live in fields or near houses, where they hunt pesky mice.

Caution! When hiking, always pay attention to any signs posted that warn of snakes in the area. Just leave the snakes alone!

RESPECT THE RATTLESNAKES PRIVACY PLEASE STAY ON THE TRAIL

Find out more
Books

Eyewitness Reptile
by Colin McCarthy
(DK Publishing, 2000)
This book covers the entire world of reptiles, of which snakes
are a big part. The book includes hundreds of photos of
amazing animals.

Snake: The Essential Visual Guide to the World of Snakes
By Chris Mattison
(DK Publishing, 2006)
Nearly 200 pages of snakes! That's what you get in this
in-depth look at snakes around the world written by a
herpetologist (that's a snake scientist, remember?).

Snakes: Perfect Pets
By Susan Schafer
(Benchmark Books, 2002)
Get a head start on having a snake as a pet in this fact-filled
book. Read about important dos and don'ts about pet snakes.

The Snake Scientist:
Scientists in the Field
By Sy Montgomery
(Houghton Mifflin, 2001)
Follow herpetologist Bob Mason as
he works to help save the red-sided
garter snake in a Canadian national
park.

Web sites

King cobras!
**www.nationalgeographic.com/features/97/kingcobra/
index-n.html**
Check out this special site about amazing king cobras from
National Geographic magazine.

A new pet for you?
www.anapsid.org/mainkids.html,
Find out if having a snake for a pet is right for you. This site
includes tips on choosing a snake and how to take care of
one as a pet.

Snakes alive!
www.enature.com/fieldguides
This nature-packed site has several sections on snakes in its
"field guides" section, including lots of pictures of different
kinds of snakes.

Drawing snakes
**http://www.enchantedlearning.com/subjects/reptiles/snakes/
printouts.shtml**
If you like to combine art with your study of nature, check
out this site, which has lots of files you can print out to draw,
color, and paint snakes.

*Note to Parents: These Web sites are not endorsed by Boy Scouts of America or DK Publishing and have
not been completely examined. However, at press time, they provided the sort of information described.
Internet experts always suggest that you work with your children to help them understand how to safely
navigate the Web.*

Glossary

Aggressive
Forceful, or ready to attack.

Ambush
To hide and attack by surprise.

Antivenom
A medicine that counteracts the effects of venom.

Bask
Lie out in the direct sunlight to heat up.

Binocular vision
Using both eyes at once. In binocular vision, both eyes look forward.

Camouflage
Coloring or patterns that help an animal blend in with its surroundings.

Clutch
A group of eggs laid by an animal at one time.

Compost
Soil formed by decomposing vegetable matter.

Concertina
An accordion-like musical instrument.

Constrict
To squeeze.

Gullet
The throat of an animal.

Habitat
The environment in which a plant or animal lives.

Herpetologist
Someone who studies reptiles and amphibians.

Hibernate
Go into a state of rest or sleep over the winter, to save energy.

Keratin
A substance that makes up hair, fingernails, cows' horns, and snakes' scales.

Membrane
In animals, a very thin layer of tissue.

Molting
The process a snake goes through when it sheds old skin to reveal new skin.

Predators
Animals that kill and eat other animals.

Prey
Animals that are killed and eaten by other animals.

Reptiles
Air-breathing animals with bony skeletons and scale-covered bodies. Like other cold-blooded animals, reptiles need outside heat to warm their bodies.

Reputation
What people think of a person or thing; how a person is regarded by others.

Serpentine
Like a snake or serpent.

Species
A group of living things that are very similar and can breed in the wild.

Tendency
Acting most often in a certain way.

Transmitters
Devices that send information electronically or by radio signal.

Tropical
Warm and moist all year.

Venom
A poisonous substance produced by some animals. The animals inject it into their enemies or their prey, usually by biting or stinging.

Vertebrae
Individual bones that are part of an animal's spine.

Vibrations
Quick back-and-forth movements.